The
Righteous Man

The Troubles of a Righteous Man

God's Provision in Tough Times

Carl Willis

Pastor of New Beginnings Christian Fellowship

Published by Carl Willis
Hoisington, Kansas

The Troubles of a Righteous Man
Copyright © 2002 by Carl Willis

ISBN 1-59196-012-6

Printed in the US by Instantpublisher.com

"Many are the afflictions of the righteous, But the Lord delivers him out of them all."

Psalm 34:19

This book is dedicated to my wife Carol and our precious children Christopher, Collin and Caitlyn. You are God's cherished treasures.

Acknowledgements

First and foremost I want to thank Jesus Christ my Lord and my Savior. Without your blood, I would be hopelessly condemned. Without your resurrection I would have no power in my life.

Thank you to Roy Savage of Central Baptist Association. You have encouraged me to write for some time. Thank you for the many words of encouragement.

Thank you to my lovely bride Carol. You share my life and brighten my every day.

Thank you to Christopher, Collin and Caitlyn. You make dad proud, just by being you.

Thank you to mom and dad for raising me in a Godly home, placing Christ at the center.

Thank you to Tim, Kelly and Maurice. You exemplify the essence of friendship.

Thank you to the folks at New Beginnings Christian Fellowship for allowing me to serve on your field.

Contents

Introduction

We often hear that God is always watching over us, but sometimes our circumstances render us blind to God's movement within our lives. As you read through the pages of this book, you will see that God's care for His children is very real and unquestionably powerful. Watch as God changes the landscape of hearts and circumstances to reveal the true love of a Heavenly Father.

The 34th chapter of Psalms has always been my favorite chapter in the Bible. But it is the nineteenth verse that has always stuck with me. It is upon the truth of this verse that I have chosen to title and write this book.

God never promised us an easy life. In fact I would say the life of a Christian is filled with intense struggles and tests of our faith. As Christians we are called to be the salt and light of the earth. Our lives should carry with them the distinction of Jesus Christ.

To live for Christ requires an awareness that trouble will always be near. The enemy looks for opportunities to cripple you and weaken your faith.

I told you that Psalms 34:19 was my favorite passage of scripture for a reason. In this one verse, God tells us that we may encounter more than our fair share of trouble. He didn't tell us it would disappear, or that He would take us around it. The promise was simple; it was a promise of complete deliverance.

The pages of this book give glimpses of God's working in my own life. The experiences detailed within are my own testimony to a very real and very loving Heavenly Father. It is my prayer that you will find encouragement and hope for your life. For there is no greater joy than walking hand in hand with Jesus each and every day. As you spend a little time walking with me, you will see that where trouble abounds, grace abounds so much more.

Chapter One

Just Enough

"The sons of Israel did so, and some gathered much and some little. When they measured it with an omer, he who had gathered much had no excess, and he who had gathered little had no lack; every man gathered as much as he should eat. "

Exodus 16:17-18

Many times when I speak about God's provision I refer to it as being "the right thing, at the right time, in just the right amount." I think of God's provision of Manna for the people of Israel as they wandered in the wilderness. There was always enough manna for today, it was always on the ground in the morning, but it could not be stockpiled. God wanted His people to rely on nothing other than His glorious provision. I have found that God has many times brought me to this place. It is in this complete reliance on God that I learn to trust Him and comprehend the fullness of His provision.

A few years ago my wife and I were preparing to celebrate our tenth wedding anniversary. We were excited about reaching this milestone and wanted to do something extra special to commemorate this occasion. We decided that we would like to go on a Caribbean cruise. Our anniversary is in early January and the weather in Southwest Kansas at that time of year is just plain cold. We poured over cruise line brochures and discussed possibilities with my uncle who was a travel agent. It was decided that we would take a seven day cruise sailing from Houston to such exotic places as Cancun, Cozumel and Roatan, Honduras. To make this grand getaway possible, my wife delivered newspapers at five o'clock each morning. Every penny she made went into a savings account set aside for this trip.

About three months prior to the cruise I had gone to Wichita, Kansas on a business trip. While I was there, I was approached by two senior managers in my company about transferring to Hutchinson, Kansas. Carol and I had felt like God was calling us to something new and recognized this move to be the direction that God would be leading us. We began to make housing preparations and found our dream home. The home was a gorgeous, early twentieth century bungalow that had been completely remodeled and had ample space for our family. The house had beautiful woodwork, ten foot ceilings and patterned hardwood floors. We knew it was the right house for us, because the dining room wall paper was the same color and pattern as our dining room chairs. We immediately signed a contract on the home and set the wheels in motion to move after returning from our cruise.

About four weeks prior to the cruise it was time to put the financing of our house in motion. Upon running the numbers we found that we were exactly eighteen hundred dollars short of covering both the closing costs for the house and having the money for our cruise. We were getting ready to increase our house payment and were not in a position to take on additional debt. Not having an easy solution in mind, I finally wound up where I should have gone to start with, on my knees. For the next week or so, Carol and I prayed each day, that God would show us His provision and His will to take care of this deficit. One Saturday evening approximately two weeks prior to the cruise, we stopped by the post office on our way home from an afternoon excursion. When Carol got the mail there was an envelope addressed to her from a local meat packing plant. Out of curiosity she opened it up to find a check for eighteen hundred dollars. Carol had applied for a job at this packing plant almost three years earlier, when we had first moved to the area. As we found out from reading the attached letter, the company had been threatened with litigation over alleged discrimination to Vietnam era veterans. The litigation covered all applicants during the previous few years. To avoid litigation, the packing plant had sent eighteen hundred dollar checks as settlement to anyone who had applied during this specified time frame, and Carol was one of those people.

An unforeseen solution coming from an unexpected place, and it was directed by the Creator of all things. Not only did God reveal that His provision was just enough at just the right time, but He taught me something else. God cares about every aspect of our lives. In the grand scheme of things going on an anniversary cruise doesn't carry much spiritual significance, but my loving Heavenly Father cared enough to make it happen.

****

The night of April 21st, 2001 is a night that will stick in our minds for years to come. Shortly after nine o'clock on the night of April 21st, a tornado nearly a quarter mile in width touched down on the outskirts of Hoisington, Kansas. By the time it went back into the clouds, it had leveled close to two hundred homes, displaced nearly one thousand people and had taken one man's life.

After initially checking on the wellbeing of our neighbors, I began calling to check on the welfare of some of the other local pastors. At about 11PM I got in touch with Maurice and Kelly. They both serve as pastors and share a love of fun, fellowship, fishing and film. They immediately offered to take my family in for the night. By God's grace the storm had passed one block to the south of their home, causing only minor cosmetic damage and roof damage. In their home they had two spare bedrooms. What started as an offer for the night, became an extended offer to remain until we were back on our feet. Over the next five months we would call these two bedrooms home, and Maurice and Kelly would become more than friends, they would become family. God would use the next five months to teach all of us the true meaning of being a part of His family. You see it didn't matter that we come from different denominations and traditions. What matters is that we are the hands and feet of Jesus.

God knew we needed a home, so He spared the home of a friend. God knew that a family of four fits comfortably into two spare bedrooms. God knew that love heals many wounds so He gave us friends. God calls us His family so He gave us a life lesson on being one.

Chapter Two

The Right Time

"Then Nebuchadnezzar the king was
astounded and stood up in haste; he said to
his high officials, 'Was it not three men we
cast bound into the midst of the fire?' They
replied to the king, 'Certainly, O king.'
He said, 'Look! I see four men loosed and
walking about in the midst of the fire without
harm, and the appearance of the fourth is
like a son of the gods!'"

Daniel 3:24-25

Like me, you have probably come to realize that very rarely are God's timing and your timing synchronized. My impatience leads to imperfection. I want it all and I want it five minutes ago. But God's perfection comes with His perfect timing. When we study the scriptures we realize that God's timing will always bring complete glory to Him alone.

Let's take a moment to ponder a few of God's greatest "on time" interventions.

- The parting of the Red Sea – Had the waters parted too late the Israelites would have been killed. Had the waters been allowed to return too soon, the Egyptians might have survived.

- The fiery furnace – Had Shadrach, Meshach and Abednego been set free prior to the furnace God's glory would not have been fully revealed. Had the angel of the Lord arrived any later, these men would have surely died.

- Peter's deliverance from jail - Peter was scheduled to be brought before

Herod the next morning and would likely face death.

As I reflect on each of these events one thing sticks out. God's perfect timing is often revealed in the midst of trials. Not before, not after, but smack dab in the middle. God fully maximizes His glory in each and every instance.

****

Have you ever had those times when you've just wished you could die? Have you ever been pushed so far that you've literally wished a lightning bolt would fall from the sky and remove you from your troubles? I think we all get to that point sometimes, whether we care to admit it or not.

One of my favorite accounts in scripture is a time of dark despair experienced by the prophet Elijah. Elijah was a mighty prophet of God, and he had seen God do many amazing and miraculous things. He had walked hand in hand with God into battles that none of us would ever care to face. Elijah had seen God move against all human odds time and time again. Yet one day Elijah hit a brick wall, because there was a price on his head. In his response, Elijah withdrew from everyone into the desert, wishing he would die. With his heart full of fear and despair, Elijah lay down and went to sleep. It was in that dark and lonely hour, that Elijah was met by God's messenger. Elijah was given the right preparations in the right amounts so that he could make a long journey. His journey would end in a one on one encounter with the Lord. Elijah needed a change of heart and focus. Elijah needed to see God.

I can relate to this event. I serve as a bi-vocational pastor which means that I support my family with a profession outside of my pastoral role. Inevitably when things get to going bad, they tend to go bad on both fronts. When I accepted the call to the pastorate of Trinity Baptist Church, I made a large professional change as well. I had been in management with a large regional bank. I had a guaranteed salary, stock options, and a nice bonus plan. For the most part we were financially comfortable. With the addition of my pastoral role, it was impractical to remain in this position with the

the bank. To better utilize my time for ministry, I gave up my management position and went to work in the investment services division of the bank. With this professional change came a move to a commission based pay structure. This transition took place in January of 2000. Just in case you've forgotten already, the stock market began to fall in March of 2000. Man's great timing rides again. Two great months of business followed by the worst bear market in thirty years. By late summer of 2000, having carried two house payments for six months coupled with a slowing economy and less than stellar commission production, our finances were taking a real beating.

Of course when it rains, it doesn't just sprinkle…it pours! During this same period of time our church was going through some major upheavals. The prominent family in our church was getting ready to move out of the area. In preparation for their move, they had stepped back from all of their roles within the church. One thing you must understand, this family had practically run the church for the past fifty years and their departure was leaving a gaping hole.

One other minor detail I should mention, we didn't have people who were ready to step up to the plate and fill the void. God had given me a definite vision and direction for the ministry of our church. I had begun actively making changes, which were not met with the greatest of reception by a few of the parishioners. Change is never a comfortable thing and a few people were struggling with the changes. Instead of sitting down with me and talking out their problems, some were choosing to air their grievances in the court of public opinion.

I was becoming horribly distraught. I had been at the church nearly a year and we were not seeing any numerical growth in the congregation. Financially my family and I were crumbling, and it seemed like the only gratitude being offered was criticism and isolation. There is something I want you to notice here. My focus was on me. Self absorption was also Elijah's problem; he had taken an inward focus. I came home one day having already cried most of the afternoon. I began to cry out at God. I'll be honest not only was I hurt, but I was angry at God for allowing me to be in this situation. I was having one grand pity party and everyone was invited. During my crying out, I told God to just take my life and get it over with. I no longer had the strength to go on. Turn out the lights and bring the show to a close.

God's ways are never my ways. God didn't take my life that day, but he did something even more incredible. He took my sorrow and my pain from me. I told Him that I needed to hear his voice and I was awestruck by His response.

I had no sooner told God that I needed to hear His voice and wouldn't you know it the telephone rang. Carol was in the room with me, as she had been given a personal invitation to attend my pity party. She picked up the phone and told me that one of my dearest friends, Tim, wanted to talk to me. Tim had been my accountability partner a few years earlier and we had developed a strong friendship. Time and career changes had separated us by distance, but we had still maintained a very close friendship. Tim was calling to give me dates for an annual day of pheasant hunting that he and I do with a few other friends each year. I no sooner spoke and he knew something was wrong. Tim began to probe into the heaviness of my heart. As I exposed the weight upon my heart to my dear friend and brother, God spoke through him. Tim's words began to penetrate my self pity and fear and before long the blindness had fallen away from my eyes. I began to see my precious Lord more clearly; He took my pain and my fear away. Tim didn't set out to heal a wounded brother, but God did. Tim had been placed in my path at just the right time.

As I hung up the phone that evening I had a renewed spirit, a restored sense of purpose, and another date to prove what lousy bird hunters this group of friends really is.

****

Sometimes God's perfect timing is not as obvious, because the problem has not become apparent. One of the things that I think will be so amazing about spending eternity with Jesus is being able to see all of the times He protected us from harm without our knowledge.

Our children had stayed with Carol's dad and his wife for a weekend. They lived in

Oklahoma City which was four hours away from us. To make trips like this easier for everyone, we would meet them in Billings, Oklahoma which was the halfway point. As we headed south out of Wichita, Kansas we heard a large "bang" underneath the front end of the car. Looking out the rear window, we saw no debris or foreign objects in the roadway. The car was not handling differently or acting strange in any manner. We continued on to Billings which was still a little over an hour away and picked up our two boys. We then drove another two hours back to Hutchinson, Kansas arriving home in time for church. We stopped by the house for a quick change of clothes and headed back to the car.

As I turned the corner from our house, the entire front of the car dropped violently. The steering wheel locked up and we skidded into the curb. When I got out of the car to see what had happened, I found the front axle broken and the entire wheel assembly separated from the car. It became apparent that the loud banging noise we had heard on our way out of Wichita earlier in the day was the front axle breaking. Incredibly, we had driven some two hundred and ten miles over the past three hours with our children in the car the majority of the way. Carol and I were both humbled realizing that had the wheel assembly separated any sooner, we would have been on the highway. As violently as the vehicle had reacted at five miles per hour, this same episode at highway speeds would have more than likely proven deadly to not only ourselves, but possibly even others. God knew we had serious mechanical problems, but God is the ultimate "Mr. Fixit." God chose the appropriate time for the whole thing to fall apart. God's timing was around the corner, close to home at five miles per hour. Our God is truly an awesome God.

****

If you've ever traveled interstate thirty five between Oklahoma City and Dallas, you know that it is a long, straight stretch of roadway with a lot of traffic and very little to see. The towns are separated by twenty mile stretches with little in between. It is most definitely not one of the better spots in this world to have a vehicle breakdown. Of course that's what happened to me one spring day in

1992. I was traveling North with my oldest son, Christopher, who was at that time, just a toddler. He and I were going to Wichita, Kansas to see my parents for the weekend. About eight miles south of Paul's Valley, Oklahoma the driver's side rear tire blew out on my sport utility vehicle. The wind was blowing strong that day and the road seemed to be filled with nothing but tractor-trailers.

I got out all of the necessities of tire changing and proceeded to go to work. Being dangerously close to the roadway I hugged up next to the vehicle as best as I could and began loosening lug nuts. With every vehicle that passed, my hair got blown around on top of my head in every direction. Once I had the lug nuts loose I set the jack and began to lift the vehicle. Almost immediately, my first problem became apparent; the vehicle supplied jack was not tall enough to sufficiently lift the rear of the vehicle so that the tire could be removed. I got back in the vehicle and reassured my son that everything would be ok. I then began looking for something to put under the jack. I found a textbook from one of my police academy classes and decided to use it for a base. I got back under the vehicle and placed the jack a second time, this time using the book as a base for added height. I began to lift the rear of the vehicle. I no sooner got the rear tire off the ground and a large truck came by and blew my vehicle off the jack. I rolled out of the way just in time as the vehicle came crashing down.

A little bit angry and increasingly frustrated, I placed the jack again. No sooner did the rear tire come off the ground and another truck came by, once again blowing my vehicle off of the jack. I was extremely distraught, so I climbed back into the vehicle and began to cry. I begged God to send someone to help. I had been amazed; one of the other highlights of this stretch of roadway is the overwhelming presence of the Oklahoma Highway Patrol. On this particular day I had not seen a squad car the whole trip. When I finished praying, I looked up in my rearview mirror and saw a pickup truck coasting up behind me. The truck had steam coming from the grill and had apparently blown a hose. The driver walked up to me and we discussed our current predicaments. He mentioned he had a large truck jack in the bed of his truck and asked me if I could give him a ride into Paul's Valley for a new hose, once we got the tire changed. I agreed and we set out to change the tire with no further delays. When we were done he climbed in to my vehicle and off to Paul's Valley we went. Within twenty minutes we had his hose replaced and we were both roadworthy again. As he and I drove off from the interstate shoulder, I was overwhelmed by God's sense of timing. Two breakdowns in the same place each having something the other needed. You may call it coincidence; I however call it a Father's love.

Chapter Three

The Right Place

"The word of the Lord came to him, saying,
'Go away from here and turn eastward, and
hide yourself by the brook Cherith, which is
east of the Jordan. It shall be that you will
drink of the brook, and I have commanded
the ravens to provide for you there."
1 Kings 17:2-4

Chapter Three ~ The Right Place

God often leads us to unique and sometimes desolate places in our lives, so that we might know Him more. The people of Israel were lead through the wilderness for forty years. God led Elijah to the brook at Cherith and to a widow's home in Zarapheth. Places of isolation and desolation where God's will was made known, and the lives of people were transformed forever.

It is in these places of desolation that God shapes and molds us into the image of Christ. I too have had my wilderness experience. For me that place also had a name...Dodge City, Kansas.

****

At nineteen years of age I had gotten passionate about pursuing a career in law enforcement. I've always been blessed by a strong sense of right and wrong. I had been fascinated by police work for years and thought of it as an exciting career choice. A year later I had relocated to Ft. Worth, Texas with Carol and our newborn son, Christopher, having taken my first law enforcement job with the Tarrant County Sheriff's Office. After five years in the

Dallas/Fort Worth area, I had gained a lifetime's worth of experience as a street cop. I had been a field training officer and a recipient of numerous awards including medals for valor and meritorious conduct. I had even been named Police Officer of the Year by the area chamber of commerce. From a professional standpoint I was set, but God was tugging on my heart, letting me know it was time to leave.

Our son was quickly approaching his fifth birthday and he would be ready to start school that next fall. As much as Carol and I loved Dallas/Fort Worth, we also realized there were better environments in which we could raise Christopher. I too was realizing that I didn't want to spend the next twenty years of my life breaking up bar fights and exposing myself to such a high degree of risk. After much prayer, Carol and I felt led to begin sending my resume' throughout Kansas, Colorado and Northern Oklahoma. I had always wanted to be a deputy sheriff with a large territory, so I concentrated primarily on county law enforcement agencies.

Chapter Three ~ The Right Place

The first department to contact me was the Boulder County Sheriff's Office in Boulder, Colorado. Oh praise the Lord...not only a Sheriff's office, but a cop job in the Rocky Mountains. What else could a guy ask for? I flew out to Boulder for my initial testing and passed. I was invited back for a second round of testing and interviews, but never returned. Living in such a beautiful place does not come cheap. During my initial visit I began pricing housing and realized that even with the substantial pay raise our family would not be able to afford the basic necessities of life. Living in such a beautiful place definitely comes with a price tag.

Soon afterward I was contacted by two more departments almost simultaneously. The first was the Ponca City Police Department in Ponca City, Oklahoma. I had lived in Ponca City as a young boy and had many fond memories of the community. Carol and I had recently gone through there on a recent mini-vacation, and she liked the community too. As I met with the recruiter, all seemed to be going along smoothly until he informed me that they were waiting on a termination appeal to be resolved. The department could not begin the hiring process until the appeal had been settled, and the settlement process would possibly take months.

The second department to contact me was the Ford County Sheriff's Office in Dodge City, Kansas. Dodge City is of course the center of the lawman universe if you are a history buff. Such great lawmen of the old west as Wyatt Earp and Bat Masterson had served in Dodge City during their lifetimes. The Sheriff's Office had recently made application to the Department of Justice for a grant under the C.O.P.s program, introduced by President Clinton in the early nineties. Their hope was to add an additional position on top of three budgeted positions they were trying to fill.

In the early part of 1995 I was called by the Ford County Sheriff's Department and asked to come to Dodge City for my first interview. I had not been to Dodge City since I was about six years old, and I only vaguely remembered Boot Hill. Dodge City was a cow town in the old west, and not much has changed in the past one hundred twenty years. As I drove into town

I was greeted by the smell of feedlots. If you're not sure what a feedlot is, let me give you a brief description. Feedlots are all you can eat buffets for cattle; a place to fatten cattle up for slaughter. As I continued into Dodge City from the Southeast I passed two meat packing plants and was greeted with all of the pleasing sites and aromas that go along with that line of business. Needless to say my first impression was that Dodge City was a dump. I went to my meeting and had a fantastic interview with a panel of five individuals, although I had pretty much made up my mind that I was only coming to the Ford County Sheriff's Office as a last option if no other possibilities existed.

I was so unimpressed with what I had seen in Dodge City that I made sure to stop by Ponca City on my way back home, just to get my face in front of them again. When I arrived home, Carol asked how my trip had gone. I told her that the last place on earth we were moving was Dodge City, Kansas. If there is one thing that I've finally picked up on in life…never say never…because God just may take you there. When the dust had finally settled and the smoke had cleared, the only offer on the table was from the Ford County Sheriff's Office in Dodge City, Kansas.

I came to Dodge City expecting to spend the next twenty years working steadily towards an early retirement at age forty-five. Soon after I got to Dodge City, I realized things were not going to be as dreamy perfect as I had planned. I was the outsider, the big city boy, and I didn't quite fit in with my rural counterparts. There were vast differences in our philosophies and work habits. I found a good old boy network that I was not likely to penetrate any time soon. Fortunately God led us to a very vibrant church. In our church we found several couples our age and I hit off an almost instant friendship with Tim, who I mentioned in the last chapter. Interestingly enough, Tim is an attorney and often did defense work. I always thought it was somewhat ironic that the street cop and the defense attorney were able to develop such a close friendship. Tim got me involved in an accountability group with several other men. We met once a week and discussed our walk with God, our relationships with family and our personal struggles. This group was a great blessing to me, for it was through their prayers and encouragement that God gave me victory in such areas of my life as my language, my attitude and my personal Bible study and prayer habits.

Our church in Dodge City was in the midst of a transition from being a traditional Southern Baptist church to being a church with a defined mission and purpose. During our years in Dodge City, I found many places to plug in, and found many mentors who were willing to take me under wing and encourage me. God used this church and the people in it to shape my passions and develop me as a Godly leader. Through the ministry of this church I was able to work with adult, youth and men's ministries as well as various other capacities. In late 1997, I felt God calling me to make a professional change. My intent was to go to work as either an administrator or trainer for another law enforcement agency. God in His infinite wisdom had far greater plans for me. The week that I was scheduled to interview with the Highway Patrol Academy, I was encouraged by a church member to apply for a job in a local bank. I would end up taking that position and as

I look back; I see where God put me in that position in order to lead me where I am today.

In May of 1998, the pastor was commenting to me that he was preparing to go on vacation, and had not yet been able to find anyone to preach for him. I felt prompted to fill in for him and offered to preach. I had preached a few times as a teenager and had at one point in my teen age years felt called to be a pastor. I had long since felt like that calling was no longer a part of my life. From the moment I offered to preach, God began making good on a young boy's commitment. Over the next year and a half he would go to work molding my heart into the heart of a pastor.

As I look back on how God has shaped my passion and method of ministry, I see much of my experience in Dodge City reflected. God allowed me to see a dynamic and bold ministry that would undertake any challenge to reach a lost and dying world with the saving message of Jesus Christ. Dodge City is now a very special place to me, for it is there that God began to call me out to fulfill His plan in my life. If you find yourself in a desolate place, you never wanted to be, take heart for it is in those places where God molds some of His greatest work.

Chapter Four

An Ever Present Help

"Then you call on the name of your god, and I will call on the name of the Lord, and the God who answers by fire, He is God."

1 Kings 18:24

Chapter Four ~ An Ever Present Help

None of us ever relishes the thought of going into battle. If you know you'll be going in alone, it is even less desirable. Yet some of God's greatest victories have been attained by an army of one plus ONE. Sometimes we forget just how mighty and powerful our Lord truly is. When God is for us, nothing will stand against us. Some of the greatest examples in the Bible were David facing off against the Philistine giant Goliath; Elijah and the four hundred prophets of Baal proving once and for all who the one true God was; and of course Samson slaying multitudes of Philistines with the jawbone of a donkey. None of these men were overly noteworthy of their own accord, but with God's anointing upon them, they were a force to be reckoned with.

****

So does God still win great victories today? You had better believe He does. On many occasions, I have seen God go before me, leading the way, and follow behind me operating as my rear guard. I am very confident of God's ever present help.

Integrity and character are two of the most sought after traits in the professional world today. Sadly though, our world cannot be described as a place of character or integrity. Almost daily we hear about the greed of people overriding their sense of decency and justice. Even as I am writing this book, hearings are being held in Washington D.C. focusing on a collapsed corporate giant. Evidence is coming to light daily that those at the top padded their pockets while thousands of employees were left holding the bag. Accountability is the next guy's problem. The last man left standing will ultimately be left holding the bag.

To be a man of character and integrity in this day and age requires that you be willing to take a stand. Taking a stand means stepping out alone. We've overlooked one important fact here, you are never truly alone. God honors our stands when they are done according to His perfect will and purpose. In my mind there is no greater honor than taking a stand for the glory of Jesus Christ.

My wife and I run an independent investment firm. A few months ago, we were approached by a local television station about doing some advertising. This particular station is affiliated with one of the three major television networks, and from a professional standpoint would be a good promotional move. The day I was supposed to meet with the advertising representative, I came across an article in a major newspaper that detailed the stance of this particular television network to move from family friendly programming. In the article the President of this particular network gave his views that racy, adult oriented programming sells and that his network would be pushing the limits with their programming. The network had seen the success of some of the more risqué programming on the cable networks, and wanted to tap into that market.

After September 11th, 2001 our business had really dropped off. Utilizing television advertising for exposure really made sense to me, but God did not give me peace about advertising with this television network. Against what would seem like sound business judgment, we called up the advertising rep and explained our reasons for not advertising with them. In my mind I could not justify someone sitting through filth and seeing my name and my face being promoted as a commercial sponsor. Ultimately I represent Jesus and making a business decision that would bring shame upon His name would be a bad decision, no matter how you looked at it.

That very next month my business enjoyed its best month since the day we opened the doors. God also provided a new means of meeting potential prospects and growing the business. I firmly believe that had I compromised my standards, God's favor would not have been experienced. Stands are often uncomfortable to make, because they set you apart. But when you really think about it, set apart is what God wanted us to be all along.

****

We moved to Hoisington, Kansas in the summer of 2000. To make friends quickly, my oldest son Christopher went to the pool each and every day. Within a few days, he had met a neighbor boy, his age, who lived just down the street from us. The very next weekend Christopher's new friend invited Christopher to spend the night. My wife and youngest son were still in Hutchinson, taking care of last minute moving issues, so it was just Christopher and I at the new house. I told Christopher to go ahead and go, and I was very excited for him to have already made new friends.

About eleven thirty that night I was out in the backyard with my dogs. While I was outside I happened to see a small shadow come across the street and towards the house. As the figure came closer, I realized it was Christopher. As Christopher came towards me, I inquired as to what he was doing home. He told me that his new friends were watching a movie that he didn't think was appropriate for him to be watching. He told me that he felt like Carol and I would not approve of the movie, so he decided to come home. I was nearly in tears as I saw character exemplified in my soon to be ten year old son. This particular night, his actions were not those of a young boy, but instead the actions of a man of integrity. Christopher had chosen to take a stand, even though it would likely cost him a friendship. As Christopher and I went inside, we discussed the fact that God had brought us here to share Jesus with those who were lost. Christopher and I took a moment and prayed for his new friend. We had no sooner finished praying and there was a knock on the front door. Christopher's new friend and the other boys spending the night had come to the house and offered to change out movies, so Christopher could come back. Christopher went back over that night and two months later, his new friend asked Jesus into his heart. God honors the stands we take, even the stand of a nine year old boy.

Chapter Five

No Storm Too Great

"He said to them, 'Why are you afraid, you men of little faith?' Then He got up and rebuked the winds and the sea, and it became perfectly calm. The men were amazed, and said, 'What kind of a man is this, that even the winds and the sea obey Him?'"

Matthew 8:26-27

One of the most frequently told Bible stories is the account of Jesus calming the storm. Jesus and His disciples were in a boat when a violent storm began. Jesus was asleep and the disciples were terrified. In a panic they woke Jesus up. He spoke to the wind and the waves causing all to turn calm. The disciples were amazed that even the wind and the sea responded to the sound of his voice.

The storms of life come in all shapes and sizes. Some storms are of the wind and rain variety, while others are man made. No matter what type of storm is bearing down on you, Jesus is there.

****

I have lived almost all of my life in an area of the country affectionately known as "tornado alley." Every year beginning in late March continuing through mid June, we go through storm season. The skies frequently rumble with thunder and the threat of nature's destructive fury is always near.

Chapter Five ~ No Storm Too Great

Throughout my lifetime I have seen many tornados. My dad was a HAM radio operator and volunteered as a storm spotter when I was a kid. I used to go out with him from time to time and was always awestruck watching the power in the winds. I was always impressed by the power these storms could unleash. Straws imbedded in telephone poles, cars thrown miles through the air, and buildings exploding. I had seen the aftermath of some of the biggest tornados in places like Andover and Hesston, Kansas.

When I became a police officer, it became my job to go out into severe weather looking for tornados. On two occasions I found them, and came much closer than I really ever wanted to come to a tornado. My first near miss occurred in Fort Worth, when a tornado passed overhead without touching down. My second occurred in Dodge City as one passed by dangerously close on the ground. Those two experiences were enough for one lifetime, but neither of these experiences prepared me for April 21, 2001.

As I alluded to in an earlier chapter, on the night of April 21st a tornado rated f-4 on the Fujita scale dropped into Hoisington, Kansas leaving a path of destruction approximately a quarter mile wide and four miles long.

Saturday April 21st was like most other Saturdays. There was work to be done around the house. My parents had come to town for the day, as my dad and I were doing some major engine work on one of our vehicles. The day had been very nice, the kind of day that makes you enjoy spring in Kansas. As the afternoon wore on, things began to change. At about five in the evening, we began to see large thunderheads building in the sky and as always during that time of the year, conditions were ripe for severe weather.

As the evening wore on, the thunderheads began getting larger and consuming the sky causing it to become eerily dark. Shortly after seven PM, my parents left to go back to Wichita and were hoping to beat the storms home. I went inside and turned on the television to see if there were any severe weather updates. There was only a severe thunderstorm watch for our area, but no other severe conditions were reported. At about eight thirty PM the winds started to get very still and reports began to come in from neighboring counties indicating that the storms we had seen building were now gaining strength.

At approximately eight forty PM another report came on the television indicating that the line of storms was now shifting direction, and it appeared that they might be coming our way. Along with this directional change, the television reported that the storms were intensifying. Reports of straight line winds in excess of sixty MPH and baseball sized hail were also beginning to come in.

Our home has numerous large windows in it. Not being overly anxious to watch baseball sized ice hit the windows at sixty MPH, I instructed my wife and kids go to the basement with some blankets and pillows in case we needed to take shelter. When you live in this part of the country, going to the basement is a typical precaution that usually turns out to be nothing more than planning for the worst.

Once we were down in the basement, we turned on the radio and began to listen to storm spotter reports that were coming in from the far western edge of the county. The sheriff called into the radio station and reported seeing a wall cloud approximately fifteen miles west of our community. Wall clouds are something that we don't like to see, because they indicate tornado producing conditions within a storm. Another report came in of straight line winds reaching speeds of nearly one hundred MPH. Shortly after this last report, the radio station got knocked off of the air. Wanting to get an update on what was going on; I decided to run back upstairs to check the radar picture on the television. Shortly after I got upstairs, I began to hear large impacts against the house, and assuming the large hail had arrived, I hurried back down stairs.

I had no sooner gotten down into the basement and the power went out. Within a matter of seconds, I heard a sound I had heard twice before, a loud unforgettable roar. This roar was different though; it was much louder than either of my other two encounters. I immediately directed Carol, who was almost three months pregnant, and my two boys under the basement staircase. When Carol asked what was wrong, I told her that a tornado was coming.

We had no sooner gotten under the staircase and the storm was on top of us. The roar of the tornado was deafening and all I could do was cry out, "save us Jesus." I heard my wife and children crying and calling upon the name of our precious Lord. In an instant windows began to shatter and my ears popped as the pressure changed. The pipes above our head and the hot water heater began to shake violently. Dust began to fall from the floor above us. All that could be heard in the roaring of the wind was the sound of breaking glass and splitting timbers. By the different noises, it was apparent that large objects were being tossed about and were striking each other with great force. My ears popped a second time as my family and I continued to cry out for God's mercy. After another twenty seconds or so, the wind began to calm, the pipes quit shaking, and the storm had passed.

God has never required eloquent prayers to bring about His response. I always think of Peter's impassioned plea of "save me!" as his water walking experience sank in a lack of focus. God had heard our prayers, simple and passionate. We needed help and we needed it quick. God had answered. We were safe, and we still had one another. We had no idea if we had anything else, but at that point it didn't matter.

As I came up from the basement, I didn't expect to find much of anything. Broken glass was all over the house and the wind was now able to blow freely throughout our home. Looking out the back door towards the north, I saw that the two homes behind me no longer had second stories. As I looked to the east at the home directly across the street, the whole front of the house was missing. Looking to the south there were homes missing their roofs and one had a collapsed porch. A forty foot tall tree that had once been the centerpiece of our yard was now pushed over against the front of the house. To the west my neighbor's home had no roof or garage and the houses going west from his were missing walls, or just plain missing. The vehicle I had been working on with my dad earlier in the day was now buried in a pile of debris. The van parked behind it had been turned at an angle and moved forward three feet.

In the morning light I would discover that our home had been the only house on our street, starting from the west edge of town and going east for five blocks that still had all of its walls and roof intact. Within a matter of months my home would be only one of approximately a half dozen or so homes in this entire area that was left standing.

While we were in the process of developing a rebuilding plan with our insurance company, a structural engineer was brought in to look at the house. I told him when he came out that he should not be shocked if he found a large God sized handprint on the roof. I fully recognized that only by God's hand of protection did our home survive and our family remain safe.

As time would pass many more stories would come to light detailing God's protection for those who called upon the name of the Lord.

Mine is only one of many, each testifying to God's presence in the midst of life's storms.

Chapter Six

Angels in Orange

"On the very night when Herod was about to bring him forward, Peter was sleeping between two soldiers, bound with two chains, and guards in front of the door were watching over the prison. And behold, an angel of the Lord suddenly appeared and a light shone in the cell; and he struck Peter in the side and woke him up, saying, 'Get up quickly.' And his chains fell off his hands."

Acts 12:6-7

Chapter Six ~ Angels In Orange

We read throughout scripture about God meeting people at their point of need in very divine and amazing ways. Two events that come to my mind are the angel of the Lord appearing in a jail cell late one night. The angel led Peter to freedom, releasing him from shackles and guards. Peter was scheduled to be put on trial the very next day. Along those same lines, the book of Acts gives the account of Phillip being led to the Ethiopian Eunuch who was searching the scriptures. Phillip was able to give the good news of Jesus Christ during this divine appointment. As soon as his work was finished God moved him.

So many times we think God doesn't work that way in people's lives anymore. I would have to disagree. The question is really this: Do you recognize God's provision for help when it comes into your life? I think sometimes we pass these divine interventions off as mere fate or chance. If we take a moment to really ponder the loving nature of our Heavenly Father, we will come to realize that they are nothing less than heaven sent.

Chapter Six ~ Angels In Orange

As I mentioned in the previous chapter, prior to the tornado of April 21st, 2001 our front yard was adorned by a forty foot tall tree. This tree was very old and measured approximately four feet thick at the trunk. During the tornado this tree was completely toppled like a domino. The force of the tornado not only toppled the tree, but pulled all of the roots out of the ground as well.

Monday April 23rd became the first day of real clean up. My dad brought his trusty home and garden sized chainsaw, as did another local pastor. Needless to say after about an hour's worth of cutting, we had made very little progress on removing this big behemoth from the yard.

As we continued cutting, something happened that I will never forget. Out of what seemed like nowhere, we were joined by a group of approximately ten people all wearing orange t-shirts, representing a large national home improvement retailer. Out of this group of ten, four were wielding large industrial sized chain saws. These folks said nothing to us; they just fired up the chain saws and went to work. Those that weren't cutting were moving large blocks of the once mighty tree and placing them by the curb. My wife joined my dad and me in the yard and we all shed some tears of gratefulness together. Within thirty minutes a yard reappeared where a tree once lay. All of the wood was stacked in a pile by the curb and as quickly as they came, they left. Not a word said, not a question asked only helping hands and willing hearts.

As they moved on to the next house my dad turned towards me and asked, "I didn't know angels wore orange son, did you?" I didn't then, but I do now.

Chapter Seven

An Endless Supply

"The bowl of flour was not exhausted nor did the jar of oil become empty, according to the word of the Lord which He spoke through Elijah."

1 Kings 17:16

One of my favorite accounts of God's provision is found in 1 Kings 17. The prophet Elijah had been instructed by God to go to Zarapheth, where he would be cared for by a widow. Upon entering the town, Elijah sees the widow and asks her to care for him. She goes on to explain that she has very little, and is in fact on her way to prepare a meal for she and her son, before they die. Elijah assures the widow that God will provide. The Bible tells us that the resources did not run out, just as God had promised.

In reading this account, I had often wondered if God still did such amazing things today. I am here to tell you, that He most certainly does. God has a plan to meet each and every need you have. When we are obedient to His will, the resources are endless.

Now before you get the wrong idea, I am not telling you that God will make you rich. I am telling you that God will provide for you in such ways that you will be awestruck by the way He works. God's ways have never been the ways of men. I'm so grateful that this is the case, because His ways are so much more impressive.

In late May of 2001, Carol and I took a trip to my favorite haven of rest, Ouray, Colorado. Ouray is nestled in between the peaks in the San Juan mountain range in Eastern Colorado. Carol and I needed a little time away to decompress and talk. We had been running non-stop since the tornado had turned our lives upside down the month before.

In addition to the all of the tornado turmoil, the bank I worked for was going through an extended "right-sizing" process. The landscape of my work environment had been carved up, trimmed and reshaped drastically over the previous twelve months.

When I first went to work for the bank's investment services group I had been assigned eleven branch banks throughout Western Kansas. By May of 2001 six of the eleven banks had been sold and the number of banks assigned to me had decreased to five. In addition the staff at my primary business location had been reduced from fifty to a little over ten. With these sweeping changes, I had seen a sweeping reduction in my business. The referrals were no longer coming in with any consistency. People were understandably more concerned about being employed than referring investment business to me.

My territory had been a new territory for the investment services division. I had to start from the ground and build up a business. I had a good friend that was a recruiter for a regional investment firm and he continued to stay in touch with me on a regular basis. He often encouraged me to consider going on my own at some point. On many occasions Carol and I had kicked around the idea of opening an independent investment firm, but we just did not feel as though we were financially ready.

Since the tornado of April 21st had come through we had seen not only the landscape of Hoisington, Kansas change, but we had seen our own financial landscape transformed as well. As damages were tabulated and settlements made, Carol and I had decided to eliminate some of our biggest monthly expenses. We had created most of these debts buying "stuff," and we felt like there were better uses of the money than just buying more "stuff." By the time all was said and done, we had eliminated a second mortgage, and two car payments. We had been praying for some time that God would allow us to get these debts paid off quickly, and with one two hundred and forty mile per hour wind, He did! In light of our new financial picture and having some savings built up, I asked my friend to mail me the recruiting materials for his company.

While Carol and I were in the mountains, we began to discuss God's course for our lives. I generally know when God is leading me to make a change, because I get very restless where I am. When it came to my work situation, I had felt this way for about four or five months.

Career changes are not as easy when you are a bi-vocational pastor. You have to weigh any career changes against the backdrop of your ministry. Always keeping in mind that the ministry is your true calling; your profession is something you do to support that calling.

Carol and I talked over our current station in life; we both felt very strongly that it was time to make a change. In reviewing the materials my friend had sent, we were very interested in what his firm had to offer. Before we left Colorado, I called my friend up and we scheduled a meeting for the next week.

Big decisions are never easy to make. I have always said there is sometimes a fine line between faith and stupidity. Knowing which side of that line you are on requires sensitivity to God's leading. Over the next few days, Carol and I would spend a great deal of time in prayer. Time with God is always time well spent. God does not play guessing games with His children; I find that His will is always clear. Trouble with discernment comes from our side of the equation, never God's.

There was an overwhelming peace about making this career move. Carol and I had been led to the same conclusion and were in complete agreement. Prior to even meeting with my friend, I went looking for office space. I had always had in my mind, should I ever go independent, that I would want my office to be located on the courthouse square. One of my clients owns a building in the general area where I wanted to locate. In fact, he had his office on the square. I sat down with him and explained what I was trying to do. One thing I should tell you first, not only is this man a client, but he is a very dynamic Christian. Almost immediately and without hesitation, he told me that I could take his office. Carol and I were both startled and if that wasn't enough, he was going to leave the fax machine, the copier and two phone lines.

On June 15, 2001 we were officially opened for business. With new furniture, a new commission structure, and a whole lot of hope for the future we moved forward. The month of June wasn't bad with only two production weeks available we were pleased with the results. July however was a different story. By the time July was over, we only had a couple hundred dollars in commission and to top it off, a mistake had been made on June's commissions. No paycheck would be available for August and of course in our family we have two birthdays during that month.

After praying about the solution, I felt led to use some of our savings to pay the expenses for the month. I felt led to invest the rest into the markets. This really defied logic. I knew we would need our savings at a later date, to pay for some of the renovations on our home. In addition, just to keep it interesting, Carol and I felt led to tithe off of our insurance settlement money and she was now six months pregnant. As I continued to seek God, I continued to get the same response, so stepping out in faith we did as we felt led.

Within a matter of days several of the investments I made had tremendous increases. Within two weeks every dollar we had taken out had been replaced. The balance of the account never changed.

On the morning of September 11, 2001 hijackers took control of four commercial jets. They would ultimately fly two of these jets into the twin towers of the World Trade Center in New York City. One of the two remaining jets ended up flying into the Pentagon in Washington, D.C. The final jet would crash into a field in rural Pennsylvania. With these acts of terror thousands of lives were lost and the United States was brought to a stand still. The stock markets closed on September 11th and did not reopen until the following Monday. Investors already nervous over the sluggish economy, decided to take a wait and see approach. My business was already off some twenty percent compared to the previous year and things didn't look good for the remaining quarter.

Just to add some additional intrigue to the whole situation. Carol and I were expecting our third child in mid October. I knew that the same God, who had been with us in the middle of the storm, would be with us again. On October 11, 2001, Carol gave birth to our precious daughter Caitlyn.

By the time 2001 had come to a close, my business ended down nearly thirty-five percent compared to the previous year. We would utilize our savings several more times to fund our family and our business. Each time,

God would replace every dollar used with another dollar of investment gain. When I did my taxes I came to find out just how truly spectacular God's provision had really been. We had withdrawn over sixty percent of our original savings balance during the last six months of 2001. My income compared to our business expenses had left a deficit of over twenty-four thousand dollars during this same time period. Yet the balance in our savings was at the same place it had been, the day we opened for business.

As I stated before, God still does great things. Times may change, people may change, but one thing remains constant. God provides for His people in ways that are beyond comprehension.

Final Thoughts

As you've read through this book you've been given a glimpse into the life of my family and me. This book is not meant to be about me, but is intended to tell of God's grace and mercy.

Ultimately we as men and women face no greater trouble than our own sinful condition. The Bible tells us that each and every one of us have sinned and fallen well short of God's glory. Our trouble comes to a head when we realize that the reward for our sinfulness is death. Not just physical death, but eternal separation from God's love; judgment that never ends.

But God had a plan to deliver each of us from this eternal judgment. That plan was Jesus Christ, His one and only son. Jesus walked this earth as a man, but yet He lived a sinless life. Jesus was a perfect sacrifice, put to death on a Roman cross to pay for my sin and yours. Jesus took upon Himself our reward for sinfulness.

Jesus' death was not the end of the story, but only the beginning. Three days after He died He stepped forth from the grave, and brought with Him the promise of a new life.

Jesus conquered death once and for all, offering eternal life to those who would put their faith in Him.

To experience the life changing grace offered in Jesus Christ simply pray this prayer:

DEAR HEAVENLY FATHER,

I ADMIT THAT I AM NOT WITHOUT SIN. I REALIZE THAT MY SINFUL CONDITION SEPARATES ME FROM YOU. I BELIEVE THAT JESUS DIED ON THE CROSS TO PAY THE PENALTY FOR MY SIN AND THAT HE ROSE AGAIN TO GIVE ME NEW LIFE. FATHER I ASK JESUS TO COME INTO MY LIFE THIS VERY MOMENT TO BE THE SAVIOR AND LORD OF MY LIFE. THANK YOU FOR LOVING ME AND SAVING MY SOUL.
AMEN